ARIZONA
COLOR ME WACKY!

GRAND CANYON STATE
PLANTS, ANIMALS,
AND INSECTS

By Conrad J. Storad & Lynda Exley
ILLUSTRATED BY MICHAEL HAGELBERG

Little Five Star

J

ohnny and
Jayne Ringo are ringtails.
They invite you to learn all about
Arizona's wacky plants, animals
and insects. The ringtail is Arizona's
official state mammal. Would you like
to know more? Get out your crayons
or colored pencils. Ready…Set…
Turn the page and have fun!

ROADRUNNERS are the world's
fastest running flying birds. They can zip across
the desert at 15 miles per hour or faster.
But guess what?
They don't really say *meep, meep.*

SCORPIONS are nocturnal.
That means they are most active at night.
Watch out for the stinger at the tip of the tail.
It can deliver a venomous sting.

COLOR ME 5 WACKY

ARIZONA is home
to more kinds of rattlesnakes than any other state.
The Western Diamondback is the biggest. It can grow up to 6 feet long!

CENTURY PLANTS bloom only once during their lifetime.
Then they die. That's true. The myth is that it takes 100 years before
they bloom. The plant usually blooms in less than 25 years.

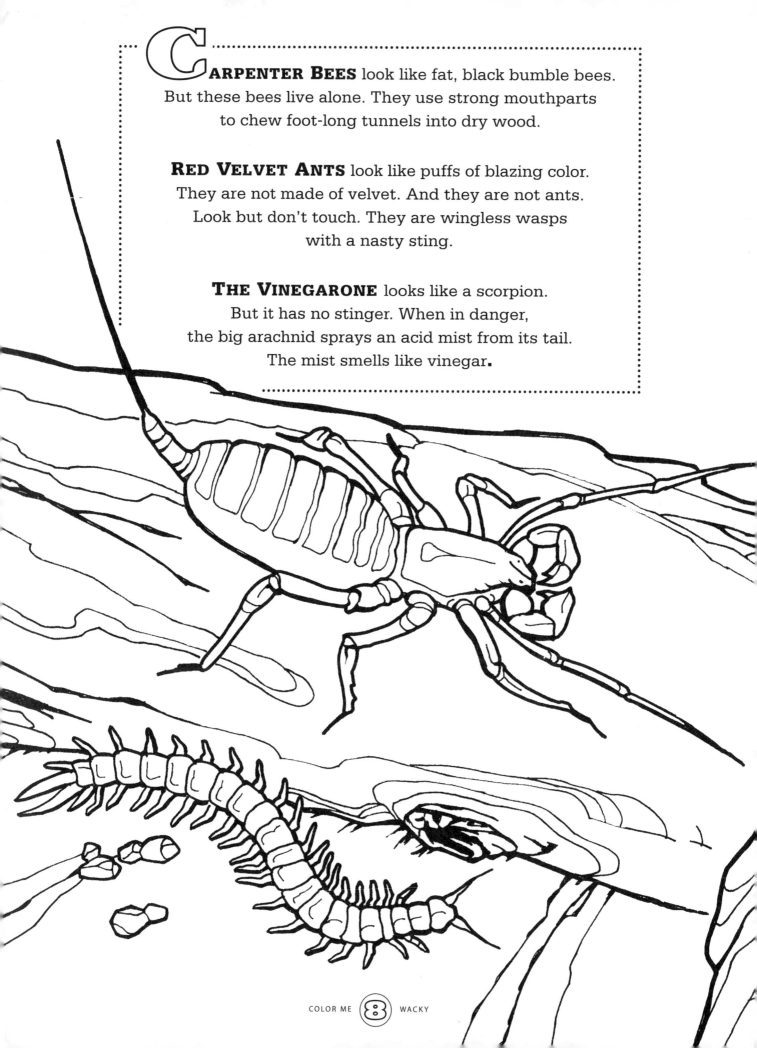

CARPENTER BEES look like fat, black bumble bees. But these bees live alone. They use strong mouthparts to chew foot-long tunnels into dry wood.

RED VELVET ANTS look like puffs of blazing color. They are not made of velvet. And they are not ants. Look but don't touch. They are wingless wasps with a nasty sting.

THE VINEGARONE looks like a scorpion. But it has no stinger. When in danger, the big arachnid sprays an acid mist from its tail. The mist smells like vinegar.

JAVELINAS are NOT wild, hairy pigs.
Please don't call them pigs.
Javelinas can weigh more than 50 pounds. They live in herds.
A favorite food is prickly pear cactus…stickers and all!

PRICKLY PEAR CACTUS grows in many places
around the world. In Arizona, prickly pear is a favorite food
for lots of animals. Some eat the fruit.
Others each the spiny pads.

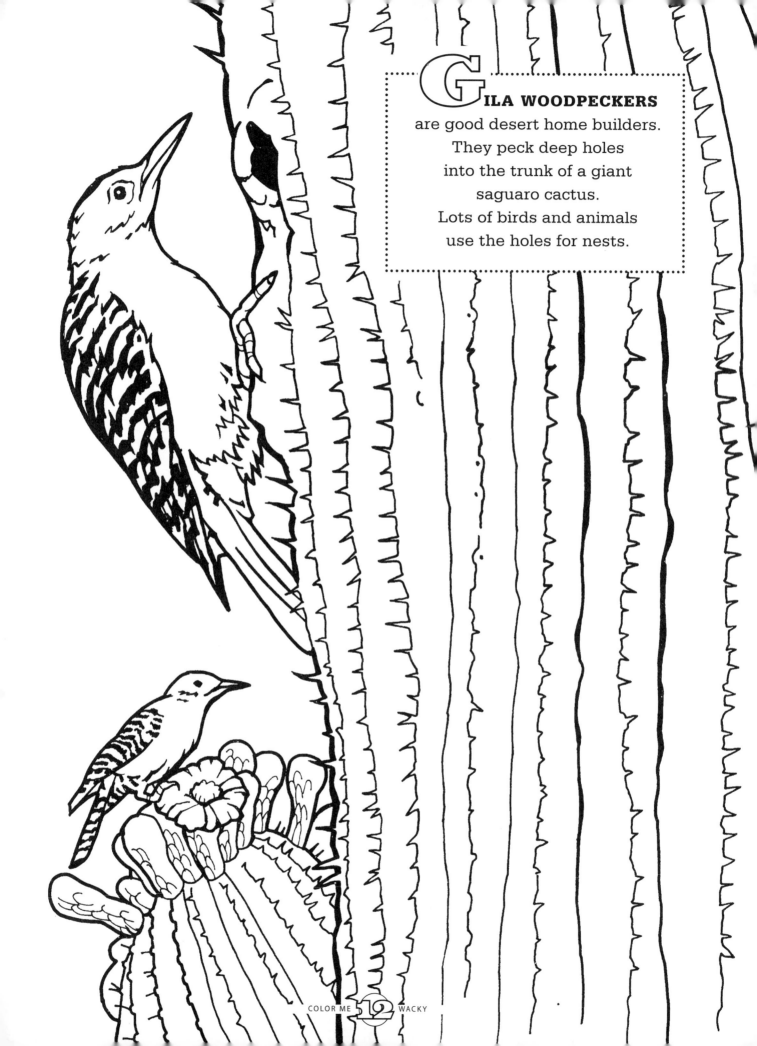

GILA WOODPECKERS

are good desert home builders.
They peck deep holes
into the trunk of a giant
saguaro cactus.
Lots of birds and animals
use the holes for nests.

THE ANTELOPE JACKRABBIT

is not really a rabbit. It's a hare. Jackrabbits can run in bursts of up to 50 miles per hour. That's much faster than you or me.

HUMMINGBIRDS
live life in the fast lane.
Some can beat their wings
as fast as 80 times per second.
In Arizona, Ramsey Canyon
is a great place
to see hummingbirds
of many kinds.

ELF **OWLS** are tiny.
They stand only 5 to 6 inches tall.
In Arizona, they make nests in
the holes of a giant saguaro cactus.
Elf owls have bright yellow eyes.

ARIZONA IS HOME to many kinds of bats.
Some of the flying mammals eat fruit. Others prefer the bug buffet.
Little brown bats can eat thousands of mosquitoes in a few hours.
That's some serious skeeter munching!

THE ARIZONA QUEEN OF THE NIGHT is an amazing plant.
You can smell its flower from more than 100 feet away.
The flower blooms and stays open for only one night.

GILA MONSTERS

are the biggest lizards in Arizona.
Some can grow 2 feet long. They are shy reptiles.
But beware! Gila Monsters have a mouth
full of sharp teeth and a venomous bite.

DESERT TORTOISES do not run from predators.
They tuck head, legs and tail into the safety of a hard shell.
When danger is gone, they come out to eat flowers
and munch on cactus pads.

THE FISHHOOK BARREL CACTUS is sometimes called
the "Water Barrel." Curved red spines protect the plant's body.
Native Americans used the sharp spines
as fishing hooks.

TARANTULAS are hairy, scary looking spiders
with two large fangs. But they are actually very shy creatures.
Desert tarantulas can grow as big as your hand. Don't bother them.
They won't bother you.

THE TARANTULA HAWK WASP hunts big spiders for food.
But not for itself. The wasp paralyzes a spider with a powerful sting.
It then lays a single egg on the living spider. When the egg hatches,
the wasp's larva has a fresh spider to eat...alive!

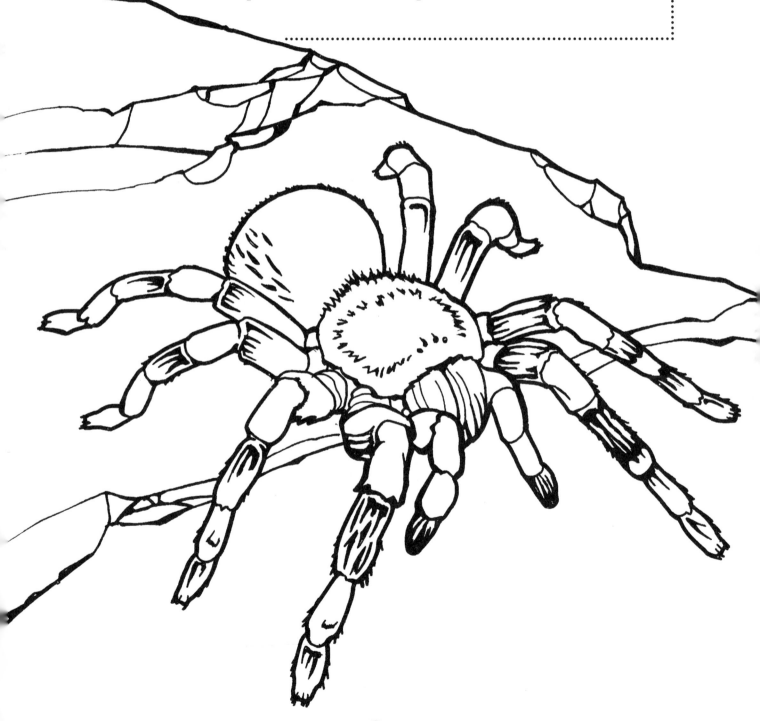

ARIZONA STATE STUFF

Saguaro Cactus Blossom
ARIZONA'S STATE FLOWER
The blossoms are creamy white.
They bloom atop the giant saguaro cactus
from May to July.

Cactus Wren

ARIZONA'S STATE BIRD

The raspy voice of the Cactus Wren
calls *chew, chew, chew*. They chatter while
they hunt for insects, spiders and lizards.

Petrified Wood
ARIZONA'S STATE FOSSIL

Arizona Tree Frog
ARIZONA'S STATE AMPHIBIAN

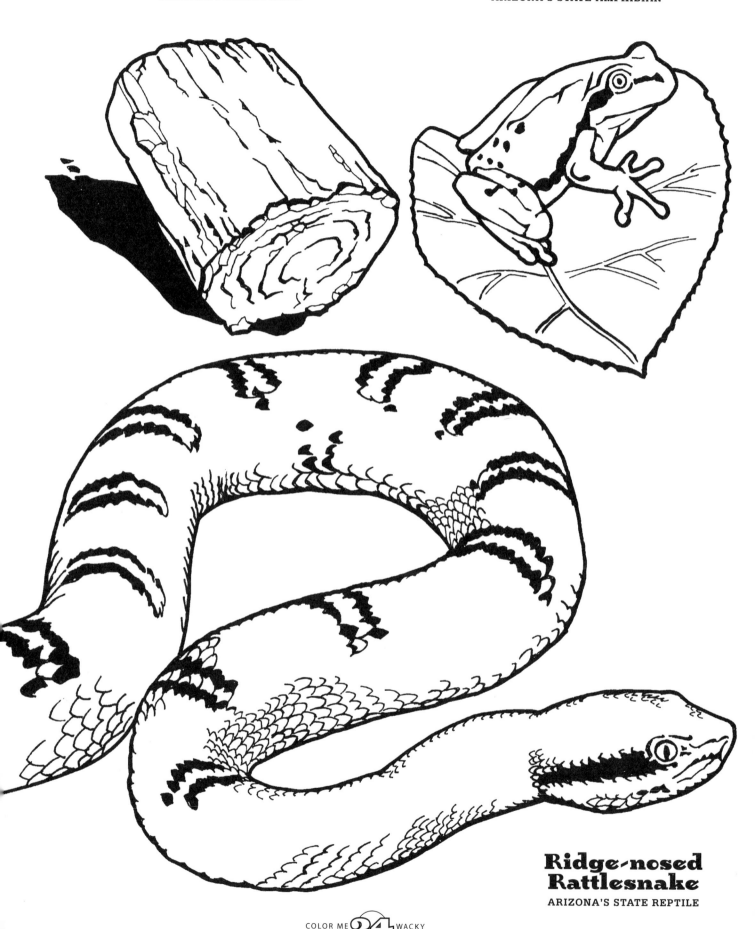

Ridge-nosed Rattlesnake
ARIZONA'S STATE REPTILE

Two-tailed Swallowtail
ARIZONA'S STATE BUTTERFLY

Ringtail
ARIZONA'S STATE MAMMAL

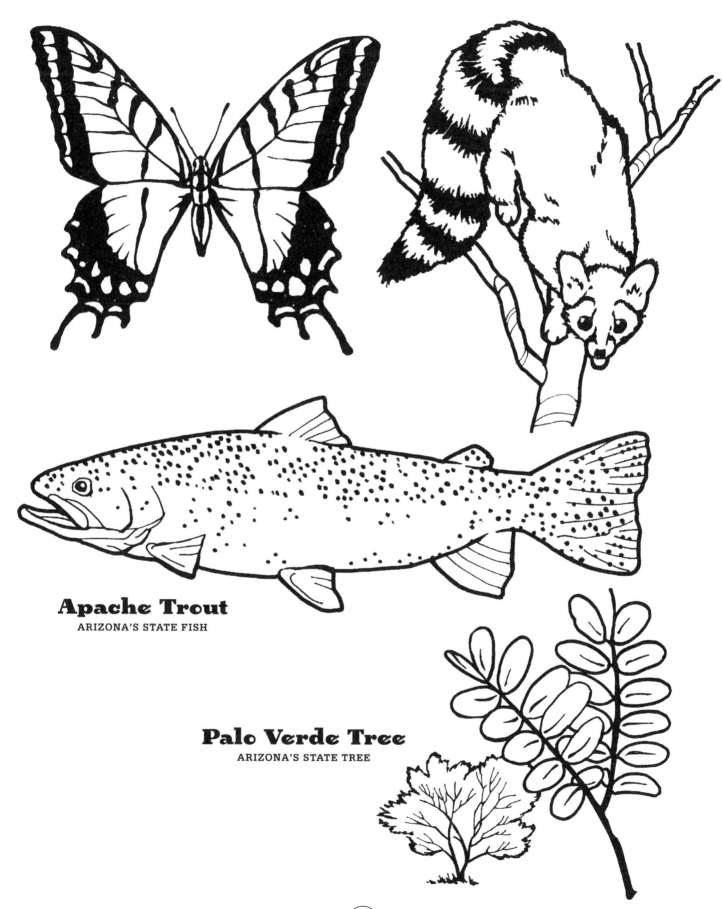

Apache Trout
ARIZONA'S STATE FISH

Palo Verde Tree
ARIZONA'S STATE TREE

GAMBEL'S QUAIL has a loud, cackling call.
Listen close. *Ka-KAA-ka-ka.* It repeats. The plump little bird
sports a black, tear-shaped plume on its head.
A group of quail is called a covey.

TIGER BEETLES have excellent eyesight, long legs,
and sharp jaws. They are speedy hunters. The beetles look
like colored jewels flashing across the desert floor
as they chase a tasty insect snack.

COYOTES love to talk.
Yep, it's true. Coyotes use at least
10 different sounds to communicate.
They bark, yip, growl and howl.
No texting for them.

BLACK WIDOWS are one of the most feared of all spiders. The females do eat their mates...but not always. They'd much rather feast on insects trapped in their tangled, sticky web.

HARRIS HAWKS

are just one of Arizona's many raptors.
The big birds often hunt in pairs.
Watch for them perched atop a telephone pole
as you drive along the highway.

ARIZONA BLISTER BEETLES have a bright orange
head and thorax. The body is blue-black.
The inch-long beetles are poisonous to many animals.
Birds learn that the bright colors mean
"Danger! Don't eat me. I taste nasty!"

Sensational Centennial Reads

Five Star Publications' *Arizona Way Out West & Wacky, Arizona Way Out West & Witty: Library Edition, Arizona Color Me Wacky!, Addie Slaughter: The Girl Who Met Geronimo* and *Cheery: The True Adventures of a Chiricahua Leopard Frog* are all designated Arizona Centennial Legacy Project books. Purchase them online at www.FiveStarPublications.com; click on "Bookstore."
To book the authors for a school visit, call 480-940-8182 or email info@FiveStarPublications.com.

Arizona Way Out West & Wacky! This 112-page book is ideal for grades K-6, offering hours of fun through true, but humorous, gross, interesting and wacky stories and facts about Arizona. PLUS: crossword puzzles, coloring pages, games, recipes, crafts, word searches and brain busters!

Arizona: Color Me Wacky! Born out of the wildly successful *Arizona Way Out West & Wacky*, *Arizona Color Me Wacky!* features 32 pages of coloring fun. The text teaches children about the Grand Canyon State's unique animals, plants and insects. The delightful, yet scientifically correct illustrations were created by award-winning illustrator Michael Hagelberg.

Arizona Way Out West & Witty: Library Edition (Chapter Book) This 116-page *ONEBOOK for Kids 2012* winner is ideal for grades 4 to adult, offering all the same entertaining and educational tales as *Arizona Way Out West & Wacky*, as well as puzzles, games, recipes, crafts and brain busters! EXCEPT *AZ-Witty* is not designed to be written in. PLUS, it includes a curriculum guide!

Addie Slaughter: The Girl Who Met Geronimo tells the true story of Sheriff John Slaughter's young daughter. In the late-1800s, she bravely travels from Texas to the Slaughter Ranch on the Arizona-Mexico border. On her journey her mother dies; she narrowly escapes from a stagecoach robbery and murder; the ranch is destroyed by earthquake ; her father's earlobe is shot off; and she meets with Geronimo. Visit www.AddieSlaughterBook.com.

Cheery: The true adventures of a Chiricahua Leopard Frog lets children read the story of this little creature growing from tadpole to frog. They learn why many kinds of frogs around the world, including those like Cheery, are dramatically declining in numbers. Visit www.CheeryAFrogsTale.com.

www.AZWOWW.com | www.AddieSlaughterBook.com | www.CheeryAFrogsTale.com